My
TRAVELJOURNAL

DATE: PLACE:

HOW I FELT TODAY:

WHAT I'VE SEEN TODAY:

_____
_____
_____
_____
_____
_____
_____
_____
_____
_____
_____
_____

WHAT I ATE TODAY:

_____
_____
_____
_____

HOW DID WE TRAVEL:

THE BEST THING THAT HAPPENED TOODAY:

_____
_____

THE WEATHER TODAY WAS:

DATE: PLACE:

HOW I FELT TODAY:

WHAT I'VE SEEN TODAY:
_____
_____
_____
_____
_____
_____
_____
_____
_____
_____
_____

WHAT I ATE TODAY:
_____
_____
_____
_____
_____

HOW DID WE TRAVEL:

THE BEST THING THAT HAPPENED TOODAY:
_____
_____

THE WEATHER TODAY WAS:

PLACE FOR DRAWINGS, PAINTINGS, WRITING, ENTRY TICKETS, PICTURES OR ALL THE OTHER STUFF YOU WANT TO CAPTURE

DATE: _____ | PLACE: _____

HOW I FELT TODAY:

WHAT I'VE SEEN TODAY:	WHAT I ATE TODAY:
_____	_____
_____	_____
_____	_____
_____	_____
_____	_____
_____	
_____	**HOW DID WE TRAVEL:**
_____	
_____	
_____	
_____	

THE BEST THING THAT HAPPENED TOODAY:

_____

_____

THE WEATHER TODAY WAS:

DATE: PLACE:

HOW I FELT TODAY:

WHAT I'VE SEEN TODAY:

_____
_____
_____
_____
_____
_____
_____
_____
_____
_____
_____
_____
_____

WHAT I ATE TODAY:

_____
_____
_____
_____

HOW DID WE TRAVEL:

THE BEST THING THAT HAPPENED TOODAY:

_____
_____

THE WEATHER TODAY WAS:

Date: Place:

How I felt Today:

What I've Seen today:

_____
_____
_____
_____
_____
_____
_____
_____
_____
_____
_____
_____

What I Ate Today:

_____
_____
_____
_____
_____

How did we Travel:

The Best Thing that happened tooday:
_____
_____

The Weather today was:

Date: _____ | Place: _____

How I felt Today:

What I've Seen today:

_____
_____
_____
_____
_____
_____
_____
_____
_____
_____
_____
_____
_____

What I Ate Today:

_____
_____
_____
_____
_____

How did we Travel:

The Best Thing that happened tooday:

_____
_____

The Weather today was:

PLACE FOR DRAWINGS, PAINTINGS, WRITING, ENTRY TICKETS, PICTURES OR ALL THE OTHER STUFF YOU WANT TO CAPTURE

DATE: PLACE:

HOW I FELT TODAY:

WHAT I'VE SEEN TODAY:

_____
_____
_____
_____
_____
_____
_____
_____
_____
_____
_____
_____
_____

WHAT I ATE TODAY:

_____
_____
_____
_____

HOW DID WE TRAVEL:

THE BEST THING THAT HAPPENED TOODAY:

_____
_____

THE WEATHER TODAY WAS:

DATE: _____   PLACE: _____

HOW I FELT TODAY:

WHAT I'VE SEEN TODAY:

_____
_____
_____
_____
_____
_____
_____
_____
_____
_____
_____
_____

WHAT I ATE TODAY:

_____
_____
_____
_____
_____

HOW DID WE TRAVEL:

THE BEST THING THAT HAPPENED TOODAY:

_____
_____

THE WEATHER TODAY WAS:

DATE: _____ PLACE: _____

HOW I FELT TODAY:

WHAT I'VE SEEN TODAY:

_____
_____
_____
_____
_____
_____
_____
_____
_____
_____
_____
_____
_____

WHAT I ATE TODAY:

_____
_____
_____
_____
_____

HOW DID WE TRAVEL:

THE BEST THING THAT HAPPENED TOODAY:

_____
_____

THE WEATHER TODAY WAS:

DATE: PLACE:

HOW I FELT TODAY:

WHAT I'VE SEEN TODAY:

_____
_____
_____
_____
_____
_____
_____
_____
_____
_____
_____
_____

WHAT I ATE TODAY:

_____
_____
_____
_____

HOW DID WE TRAVEL:

THE BEST THING THAT HAPPENED TOODAY:

_____
_____

THE WEATHER TODAY WAS:

DATE: _____   PLACE: _____

HOW I FELT TODAY:

WHAT I'VE SEEN TODAY:

_____
_____
_____
_____
_____
_____
_____
_____
_____
_____
_____

WHAT I ATE TODAY:

_____
_____
_____
_____
_____

HOW DID WE TRAVEL:

THE BEST THING THAT HAPPENED TOODAY:

_____
_____

THE WEATHER TODAY WAS:

DATE: _____   PLACE: _____

HOW I FELT TODAY:

WHAT I'VE SEEN TODAY:
_____
_____
_____
_____
_____
_____
_____
_____
_____
_____
_____
_____

WHAT I ATE TODAY:
_____
_____
_____
_____
_____

HOW DID WE TRAVEL:

THE BEST THING THAT HAPPENED TOODAY:
_____
_____

THE WEATHER TODAY WAS:

PLACE FOR DRAWINGS, PAINTINGS, WRITING, ENTRY TICKETS, PICTURES OR ALL THE OTHER STUFF YOU WANT TO CAPTURE

DATE:

PLACE:

HOW I FELT TODAY:

WHAT I'VE SEEN TODAY:

_____
_____
_____
_____
_____
_____
_____
_____
_____
_____
_____
_____
_____

WHAT I ATE TODAY:

_____
_____
_____
_____
_____

HOW DID WE TRAVEL:

THE BEST THING THAT HAPPENED TOODAY:

_____
_____

THE WEATHER TODAY WAS:

DATE: _____ PLACE: _____

HOW I FELT TODAY:

WHAT I'VE SEEN TODAY:

_____
_____
_____
_____
_____
_____
_____
_____
_____
_____
_____
_____

WHAT I ATE TODAY:

_____
_____
_____
_____
_____

HOW DID WE TRAVEL:

THE BEST THING THAT HAPPENED TOODAY:
_____
_____

THE WEATHER TODAY WAS:

PLACE FOR DRAWINGS, PAINTINGS, WRITING, ENTRY TICKETS, PICTURES OR ALL THE OTHER STUFF YOU WANT TO CAPTURE

Date: Place:

How I felt Today:

What I've Seen today:

_____
_____
_____
_____
_____
_____
_____
_____
_____
_____
_____
_____

What I Ate Today:

_____
_____
_____
_____

How did we Travel:

The Best Thing that happened tooday:

_____
_____

The Weather today was:

Date: .... Place: ....

How I felt Today:

What I've Seen today:

_____
_____
_____
_____
_____
_____
_____
_____
_____
_____
_____
_____

What I Ate Today:

_____
_____
_____
_____
_____

How did we Travel:

The Best Thing that happened tooday:

_____
_____

The Weather today was:

DATE: .... PLACE: ....

HOW I FELT TODAY:

WHAT I'VE SEEN TODAY:

_____
_____
_____
_____
_____
_____
_____
_____
_____
_____
_____
_____
_____

WHAT I ATE TODAY:

_____
_____
_____
_____
_____

HOW DID WE TRAVEL:

THE BEST THING THAT HAPPENED TOODAY:

_____
_____

THE WEATHER TODAY WAS:

PLACE FOR DRAWINGS, PAINTINGS, WRITING, ENTRY TICKETS, PICTURES OR ALL THE OTHER STUFF YOU WANT TO CAPTURE

Date: .... Place: ....

How I felt Today:

What I've Seen today:

_____
_____
_____
_____
_____
_____
_____
_____
_____
_____
_____
_____

What I Ate Today:

_____
_____
_____
_____
_____

How did we Travel:

The Best Thing that happened tooday:

_____
_____

THe Weather today was:

DATE: PLACE:

HOW I FELT TODAY:

WHAT I'VE SEEN TODAY:

_____
_____
_____
_____
_____
_____
_____
_____
_____
_____
_____

WHAT I ATE TODAY:

_____
_____
_____
_____
_____

HOW DID WE TRAVEL:

THE BEST THING THAT HAPPENED TOODAY:
_____
_____

THE WEATHER TODAY WAS:

DATE: _____ PLACE: _____

HOW I FELT TODAY:

😀 🙂 😐 😍 😎 😞

WHAT I'VE SEEN TODAY:

_____
_____
_____
_____
_____
_____
_____
_____
_____
_____
_____

WHAT I ATE TODAY:

_____
_____
_____
_____

HOW DID WE TRAVEL:

THE BEST THING THAT HAPPENED TOODAY:

_____
_____

THE WEATHER TODAY WAS:

Date: Place:

How I felt Today:

What I've Seen today:

_____
_____
_____
_____
_____
_____
_____
_____
_____
_____
_____
_____

What I Ate Today:

_____
_____
_____
_____
_____

How did we Travel:

The Best Thing that happened tooday:

_____
_____

The Weather today was:

Date: .... Place: ....

How I felt Today:

What I've Seen today:

_____
_____
_____
_____
_____
_____
_____
_____
_____
_____
_____
_____

What I Ate Today:

_____
_____
_____
_____
_____

How did we Travel:

The Best Thing that happened tooday:

_____
_____

The Weather today was:

DATE: _____ PLACE: _____

HOW I FELT TODAY:

WHAT I'VE SEEN TODAY:

_____
_____
_____
_____
_____
_____
_____
_____
_____
_____
_____

WHAT I ATE TODAY:

_____
_____
_____
_____
_____

HOW DID WE TRAVEL:

THE BEST THING THAT HAPPENED TOODAY:

_____
_____

THE WEATHER TODAY WAS:

Date: Place:

How I felt Today:

What I've Seen today:

_____
_____
_____
_____
_____
_____
_____
_____
_____
_____
_____

What I Ate Today:

_____
_____
_____
_____

How did we Travel:

The Best Thing that happened tooday:

_____
_____

The Weather today was:

DATE: PLACE:

HOW I FELT TODAY:

WHAT I'VE SEEN TODAY:

_____
_____
_____
_____
_____
_____
_____
_____
_____
_____
_____

WHAT I ATE TODAY:

_____
_____
_____
_____
_____

HOW DID WE TRAVEL:

THE BEST THING THAT HAPPENED TOODAY:
_____
_____

THE WEATHER TODAY WAS:

DATE: _____ PLACE: _____

HOW I FELT TODAY:

😀 🙂 😐 😍 😎 😔

WHAT I'VE SEEN TODAY:

_____
_____
_____
_____
_____
_____
_____
_____
_____
_____
_____
_____
_____

WHAT I ATE TODAY:

_____
_____
_____
_____
_____

HOW DID WE TRAVEL:

THE BEST THING THAT HAPPENED TOODAY:

_____
_____

THE WEATHER TODAY WAS:

☀️ ☁️ ⛈️ 🌧️ 🌨️

PLACE FOR DRAWINGS, PAINTINGS, WRITING, ENTRY TICKETS, PICTURES OR ALL THE OTHER STUFF YOU WANT TO CAPTURE

Date: | Place:

How I felt Today:

What I've Seen today:	What I Ate Today:
_____	_____
_____	_____
_____	_____
_____	_____
_____	_____
_____	How did we Travel:
_____	
_____	
_____	
_____	
_____	

The Best Thing that happened tooday:

_____

_____

The Weather today was:

DATE: _____ PLACE: _____

HOW I FELT TODAY:

WHAT I'VE SEEN TODAY:

_____
_____
_____
_____
_____
_____
_____
_____
_____
_____
_____
_____
_____

WHAT I ATE TODAY:

_____
_____
_____
_____
_____

HOW DID WE TRAVEL:

THE BEST THING THAT HAPPENED TOODAY:

_____
_____

THE WEATHER TODAY WAS:

DATE: PLACE:

HOW I FELT TODAY:

WHAT I'VE SEEN TODAY:	WHAT I ATE TODAY:
_____	_____
_____	_____
_____	_____
_____	_____
_____	_____
_____	**HOW DID WE TRAVEL:**
_____	
_____	
_____	
_____	
_____	

THE BEST THING THAT HAPPENED TOODAY:
_____
_____

THE WEATHER TODAY WAS:

Date: .... Place: ....

How I felt Today:

What I've Seen today:	What I Ate Today:
_____	_____
_____	_____
_____	_____
_____	_____
_____	_____
_____	How did we Travel:
_____	
_____	
_____	
_____	

The Best Thing that happened tooday:
_____
_____

THe Weather today was:

DATE: _____ PLACE: _____

HOW I FELT TODAY:

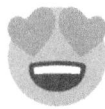

WHAT I'VE SEEN TODAY:

_____
_____
_____
_____
_____
_____
_____
_____
_____
_____
_____
_____
_____

WHAT I ATE TODAY:

_____
_____
_____
_____
_____

HOW DID WE TRAVEL:

THE BEST THING THAT HAPPENED TOODAY:

_____
_____

THE WEATHER TODAY WAS:

Date: .... Place: ....

How I felt Today:

What I've Seen today:	What I Ate Today:
_____	_____
_____	_____
_____	_____
_____	_____
_____	_____
_____	**How did we Travel:**
_____	
_____	
_____	
_____	
_____	

The Best Thing that happened tooday:
_____
_____

The Weather today was:

Date: | Place:

How I felt Today:

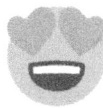

What I've Seen today:

_____
_____
_____
_____
_____
_____
_____
_____
_____
_____
_____
_____

What I Ate Today:

_____
_____
_____
_____
_____

How did we Travel:

The Best Thing that happened tooday:

_____
_____

THe Weather today was:

Date: _____   Place: _____

How I felt Today:

What I've Seen today:

_____
_____
_____
_____
_____
_____
_____
_____
_____
_____
_____

What I Ate Today:

_____
_____
_____
_____
_____

How did we Travel:

The Best Thing that happened tooday:

_____
_____

The Weather today was:

Date: Place:

How I felt Today:

What I've Seen today:

_____
_____
_____
_____
_____
_____
_____
_____
_____
_____
_____

What I Ate Today:

_____
_____
_____
_____

How did we Travel:

The Best Thing that happened tooday:

_____
_____

The Weather today was:

Date: | Place:

How I felt Today:

What I've Seen today:	What I Ate Today:
_____	_____
_____	_____
_____	_____
_____	_____
_____	_____
_____	
_____	How did we Travel:
_____	
_____	
_____	
_____	
_____	

The Best Thing that happened tooday:

_____

_____

THe Weather today was:

DATE: PLACE:

HOW I felt Today:

WHAT I'VE SEEN today: WHAT I ATE Today:

_____   _____

_____   _____

_____   _____

_____   _____

_____   _____

_____

_____   HOW DID WE TRAVEL:

_____

_____

_____

_____

THE BEST THING that happened tooday:

_____

_____

THE WEATHER today was:

Date: .... Place: ....

How I felt Today:

😀 🙂 😐 🥰 😎 😣

What I've Seen today:	What I Ate Today:
_____	_____
_____	_____
_____	_____
_____	_____
_____	_____
_____	**How did we Travel:**
_____	
_____	
_____	
_____	

The Best Thing that happened tooday:
_____
_____

The Weather today was:

PLACE FOR DRAWINGS, PAINTINGS, WRITING, ENTRY TICKETS, PICTURES OR ALL THE OTHER STUFF YOU WANT TO CAPTURE

DATE: PLACE:

HOW I FELT TODAY:

😃 🙂 😐 😍 😎 😩

WHAT I'VE SEEN TODAY:

_____
_____
_____
_____
_____
_____
_____
_____
_____
_____
_____

WHAT I ATE TODAY:

_____
_____
_____
_____

HOW DID WE TRAVEL:

THE BEST THING THAT HAPPENED TOODAY:

_____
_____

THE WEATHER TODAY WAS:

DATE: PLACE:

HOW I FELT TODAY:

WHAT I'VE SEEN TODAY: WHAT I ATE TODAY:

_____   _____
_____   _____
_____   _____
_____   _____
_____   _____
_____
_____   HOW DID WE TRAVEL:
_____
_____
_____
_____
_____

THE BEST THING THAT HAPPENED TOODAY:
_____
_____

THE WEATHER TODAY WAS:

DATE: _____ PLACE: _____

HOW I FELT TODAY:

WHAT I'VE SEEN TODAY:

_____
_____
_____
_____
_____
_____
_____
_____
_____
_____
_____
_____

WHAT I ATE TODAY:

_____
_____
_____
_____

HOW DID WE TRAVEL:

THE BEST THING THAT HAPPENED TOODAY:

_____
_____

THE WEATHER TODAY WAS:

DATE: PLACE:

HOW I FELT TODAY:

WHAT I'VE SEEN TODAY: WHAT I ATE TODAY:

_____   _____
_____   _____
_____   _____
_____   _____
_____   _____
_____

_____   HOW DID WE TRAVEL:
_____
_____
_____
_____
_____

THE BEST THING THAT HAPPENED TOODAY:
_____
_____

THE WEATHER TODAY WAS:

PLACE FOR DRAWINGS, PAINTINGS, WRITING, ENTRY TICKETS, PICTURES OR ALL THE OTHER STUFF YOU WANT TO CAPTURE

DATE: PLACE:

HOW I FELT TODAY:

WHAT I'VE SEEN TODAY:

_____
_____
_____
_____
_____
_____
_____
_____
_____
_____
_____
_____

WHAT I ATE TODAY:

_____
_____
_____
_____
_____

HOW DID WE TRAVEL:

THE BEST THING THAT HAPPENED TOODAY:

_____
_____

THE WEATHER TODAY WAS:

DATE: PLACE:

HOW I FELT TODAY:

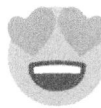

WHAT I'VE SEEN TODAY:

_____
_____
_____
_____
_____
_____
_____
_____
_____
_____
_____

WHAT I ATE TODAY:

_____
_____
_____
_____

HOW DID WE TRAVEL:

THE BEST THING THAT HAPPENED TOODAY:
_____
_____

THE WEATHER TODAY WAS:

Date: Place:

How I felt Today:

What I've Seen today:

_____
_____
_____
_____
_____
_____
_____
_____
_____
_____
_____
_____

What I Ate Today:

_____
_____
_____
_____
_____

How did we Travel:

The Best Thing that happened tooday:

_____
_____

The Weather today was:

DATE: PLACE:

HOW I FELT TODAY:

WHAT I'VE SEEN TODAY:

_____
_____
_____
_____
_____
_____
_____
_____
_____
_____
_____
_____

WHAT I ATE TODAY:

_____
_____
_____
_____
_____

HOW DID WE TRAVEL:

THE BEST THING THAT HAPPENED TOODAY:

_____
_____

THE WEATHER TODAY WAS:

DATE: .... PLACE: ....

HOW I FELT TODAY:

WHAT I'VE SEEN TODAY:

WHAT I ATE TODAY:

HOW DID WE TRAVEL:

THE BEST THING THAT HAPPENED TOODAY:

THE WEATHER TODAY WAS:

PLACE FOR DRAWINGS, PAINTINGS, WRITING, ENTRY TICKETS, PICTURES OR ALL THE OTHER STUFF YOU WANT TO CAPTURE

DATE: PLACE:

HOW I FELT TODAY:

WHAT I'VE SEEN TODAY:

_____
_____
_____
_____
_____
_____
_____
_____
_____
_____
_____

WHAT I ATE TODAY:

_____
_____
_____
_____

HOW DID WE TRAVEL:

THE BEST THING THAT HAPPENED TOODAY:
_____
_____

THE WEATHER TODAY WAS:

DATE: PLACE:

HOW I FELT TODAY:

WHAT I'VE SEEN TODAY: WHAT I ATE TODAY:

_____   _____
_____   _____
_____   _____
_____   _____
_____   _____
_____
_____   HOW DID WE TRAVEL:
_____
_____
_____
_____
_____

THE BEST THING THAT HAPPENED TOODAY:
_____
_____

THE WEATHER TODAY WAS:

DATE: PLACE:

HOW I FELT TODAY:

WHAT I'VE SEEN TODAY:

_____
_____
_____
_____
_____
_____
_____
_____
_____
_____
_____
_____

WHAT I ATE TODAY:

_____
_____
_____
_____

HOW DID WE TRAVEL:

THE BEST THING THAT HAPPENED TOODAY:

_____
_____

THE WEATHER TODAY WAS:

PLACE FOR DRAWINGS, PAINTINGS, WRITING, ENTRY TICKETS, PICTURES OR ALL THE OTHER STUFF YOU WANT TO CAPTURE

DATE: PLACE:

HOW I FELT TODAY:

WHAT I'VE SEEN TODAY:

_____
_____
_____
_____
_____
_____
_____
_____
_____
_____
_____
_____

WHAT I ATE TODAY:

_____
_____
_____
_____

HOW DID WE TRAVEL:

THE BEST THING THAT HAPPENED TOODAY:

_____
_____

THE WEATHER TODAY WAS:

DATE: PLACE:

How I felt Today:

What I've Seen today:

_____
_____
_____
_____
_____
_____
_____
_____
_____
_____
_____
_____

What I Ate Today:

_____
_____
_____
_____
_____

How did we Travel:

The Best Thing that happened tooday:

_____
_____

The Weather today was:

Date: _____ Place: _____

How I felt Today:

What I've Seen today:	What I Ate Today:
_____	_____
_____	_____
_____	_____
_____	_____
_____	_____
_____	How did we Travel:
_____	
_____	
_____	
_____	
_____	

The Best Thing that happened tooday:

_____

_____

The Weather today was:

Date: _____ Place: _____

How I felt Today:

What I've Seen today:

_____
_____
_____
_____
_____
_____
_____
_____
_____
_____
_____
_____

What I Ate Today:

_____
_____
_____
_____
_____

How did we Travel:

The Best Thing that happened tooday:

_____
_____

The Weather today was:

DATE: PLACE:

HOW I FELT TODAY:

WHAT I'VE SEEN TODAY:

_____
_____
_____
_____
_____
_____
_____
_____
_____
_____
_____
_____
_____

WHAT I ATE TODAY:

_____
_____
_____
_____
_____

HOW DID WE TRAVEL:

THE BEST THING THAT HAPPENED TOODAY:
_____
_____

THE WEATHER TODAY WAS:

Date: Place:

How I felt Today:

What I've Seen today:

_____
_____
_____
_____
_____
_____
_____
_____
_____
_____
_____
_____

What I Ate Today:

_____
_____
_____
_____

How did we Travel:

The Best Thing that happened tooday:

_____
_____

The Weather today was:

Date: Place:

How I felt Today:

What I've Seen today: What I Ate Today:

_____   _____
_____   _____
_____   _____
_____   _____
_____   _____
_____
_____   How did we Travel:
_____
_____
_____
_____

The Best Thing that happened tooday:
_____
_____

THe Weather today was:

DATE: PLACE:

HOW I FELT TODAY:

WHAT I'VE SEEN TODAY:

_____
_____
_____
_____
_____
_____

_____
_____
_____
_____
_____
_____

WHAT I ATE TODAY:

_____
_____
_____
_____
_____

HOW DID WE TRAVEL:

THE BEST THING THAT HAPPENED TOODAY:

_____
_____

THE WEATHER TODAY WAS:

DATE: _____ PLACE: _____

HOW I FELT TODAY:

WHAT I'VE SEEN TODAY:

_____
_____
_____
_____
_____
_____
_____
_____
_____
_____
_____
_____

WHAT I ATE TODAY:

_____
_____
_____
_____
_____

HOW DID WE TRAVEL:

THE BEST THING THAT HAPPENED TOODAY:

_____
_____

THE WEATHER TODAY WAS:

jonathan kuhla
tempelhofer ufer 15
109 63 berlin
mail: jonathankuhla@gmail.com

Printed in Dunstable, United Kingdom